I Watch Flies

by GLADYS CONKLIN

pictures by JEAN ZALLINGER

Holiday House · New York

A companion volume to
I LIKE BEETLES
I LIKE BUTTERFLIES
I LIKE CATERPILLARS
WE LIKE BUGS

Library of Congress Cataloging in Publication Data

Conklin, Gladys Plemon.
   I watch flies.

   SUMMARY: A child describes the appearance and
activities of a wide variety of flies.
   1.   Flies—Juvenile literature. [1.   Flies]
I. Zallinger, Jean Day. II. Title.
QL533.2.C66   595.7'7   76–26532
ISBN 0-8234-0290-8

To Melinda,
who is always
"full of 'satiable curiosity"

Some people hate flies
but I think they're interesting.
Many of them have beautiful
colors. They come in all
kinds of shapes and sizes.
Some of them bite
but others don't. Lots of flies
are good and some are bad.
I think all flies are interesting.

BEE FLY
DROPPING
ITS EGGS

I like to watch a bee fly hovering.
It hangs in the air as though
it's on a string. Its wings beat
so fast that I can't see them.
Suddenly it isn't there.
It flies so fast
that I didn't see it leave.

BEE FLIES

BLACKFLY I ACTUAL LENGTH OF FLY

One morning we went fishing.
Near the water, the air was
full of little black flies.
They crawled up my sleeves
and around my neck.
They were hunting for blood
and they found mine.
Their bites don't hurt but they itch.

On warm sunny days
I listen for the blowflies.
They make a loud buzzing sound
that my mother doesn't like to hear.
They're twice as big as houseflies
and a brilliant green color.
They're hunting for meat
they can lay their eggs on.

BLOWFLY
GREENBOTTLE FLY

CRANE
FLY

I don't like to pick up
crane flies. They don't bite
but their long delicate legs
fall off in my hands.
As the sun goes down,
I run to the pond to watch them.
They gather in little swarms
in the air and dance up and down.

SNIPE FLY

I

Snipe flies have a sharp bite and they
suck blood. The females gather
in big clusters on plants that grow
at the edge of the water. They lay
their eggs in heavy bunches
hanging over the water. The Indians
used to collect the eggs for food.

A large bowl of fresh fruit
is always on our kitchen table.
On my way outdoors
I reached for a ripe apricot.
It was covered with tiny
yellow flies with red eyes.
Where did they come from?
They weren't there yesterday.

FRUIT
FLY
I

In the summer, little swarms of
dance flies gather down by the pond.
They move up and down in a
courtship dance. A male catches
a little fly and offers it to a female.
Sometimes he puts it
in a little balloon he makes.
If she eats it, they leave the crowd
and go off together to mate.

DANCE FLY ⊢

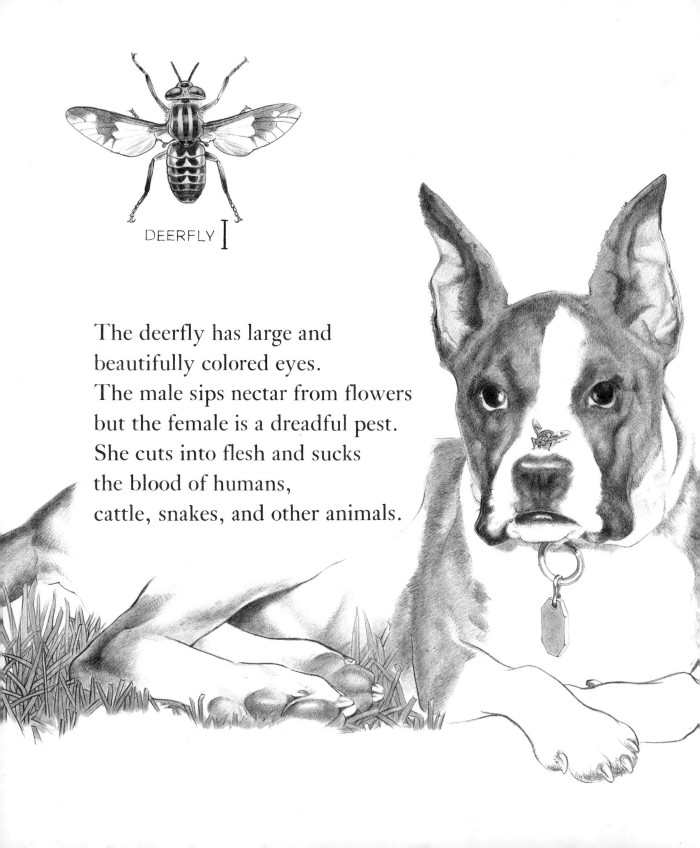

DEERFLY I

The deerfly has large and
beautifully colored eyes.
The male sips nectar from flowers
but the female is a dreadful pest.
She cuts into flesh and sucks
the blood of humans,
cattle, snakes, and other animals.

GALLFLY

Sometimes goldenrods have little
swellings on the stems.
They're called galls.
I picked one and put it in a jar.
One morning there was
a little fly there.
The swelling had a tiny hole in it,
where the fly came out.
I'll take the jar outside and let the
beautiful little gallfly go free.

HORSEFLY

On my grandfather's farm
there are big black horseflies.
It's the female who bites the horse
and sucks the blood. Her bite is sharp
and fiery and she sucks for a long time.

Houseflies are dangerous pests.
They carry germs on their feet
and then they walk on our food.
They have sticky pads
on the bottoms of their feet.
That's why they can walk
upside down across the ceiling.

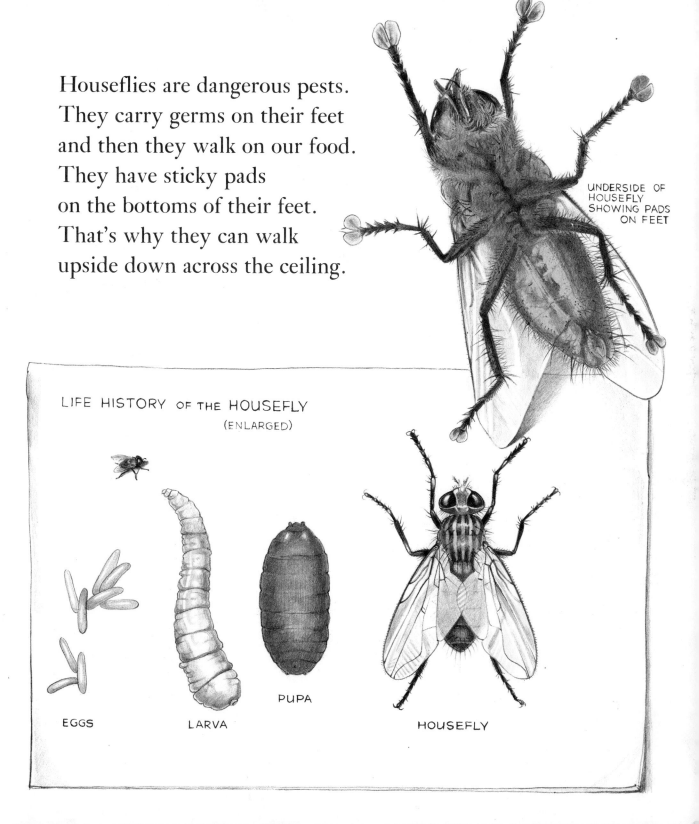

UNDERSIDE OF
HOUSEFLY
SHOWING PADS
ON FEET

LIFE HISTORY OF THE HOUSEFLY
(ENLARGED)

EGGS

LARVA

PUPA

HOUSEFLY

The hover fly is like a tiny helicopter.
It can stay in one spot in the air
for a long time. I can't see the wings
because they beat so fast. As I watch
a hover fly, it suddenly disappears.
A moment later it's back.
I didn't see it coming.
How does it move so fast?

HOVER FLY

MIDGE I

Midges are very tiny flies
about the size of mosquitoes.
Most of them don't bite.
But one kind gets into my hair,
all around my face, and bites hard.
I run into the house
to get away from them.
My mother calls them "no-see-ums."

Real flies have only two wings.
Other flying insects have four.
The mosquito is a fly because it has
only two of them. Sometimes its bite
makes people very sick. Only the females
bite and suck your blood.
They have to have a meal of blood
or they can't make any eggs.

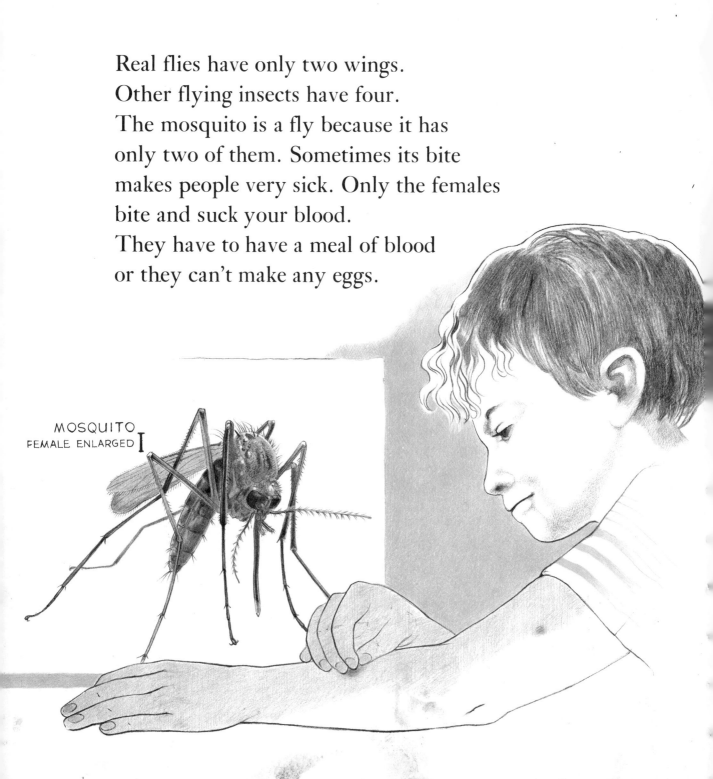

MOSQUITO
FEMALE ENLARGED

The fierce robber fly sounds like
a bee buzzing when it flies
past me. It can hang in the air
in one spot as though it were
hanging on a string.
When a dragonfly passes by,
the robber fly swoops down
and carries it to the ground
to make a meal of it.

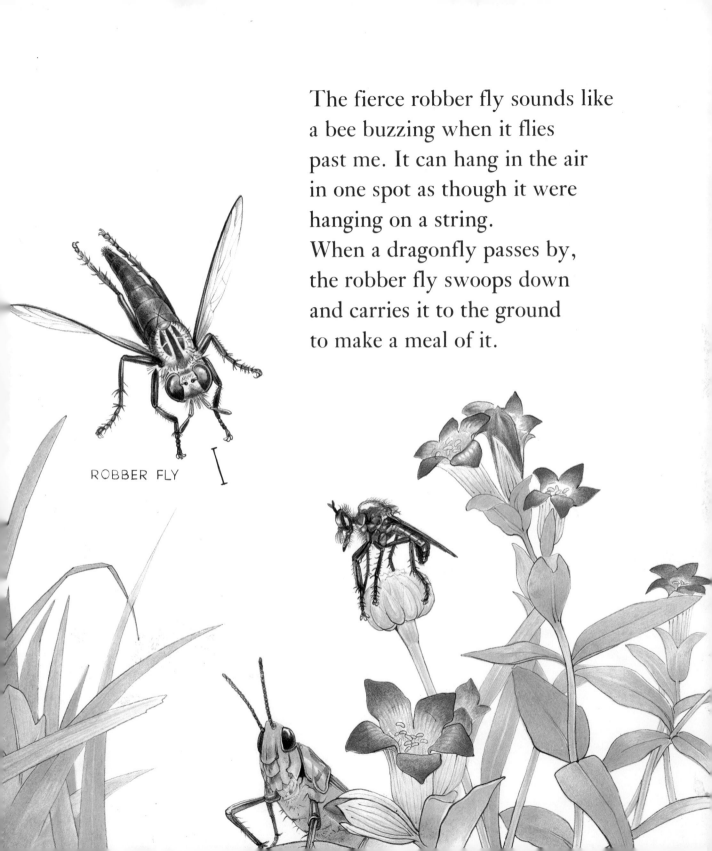

ROBBER FLY

STABLE FLY

If a fly in the house bites me,
I know it isn't a housefly.
They don't bite.
It might be a stable fly that
came into the house by mistake.
It doesn't like our food. It likes
the sweet nectar it finds in flowers.
But most of all it likes blood.

Many tachina flies lay their eggs
on caterpillars. When the eggs hatch,
the little tachina larvas
eat their way into the big caterpillar
and feed inside of it. My father
showed me a tachina fly in our
garden. He said it was a good fly
because it killed a lot of caterpillars
that were eating our vegetables.

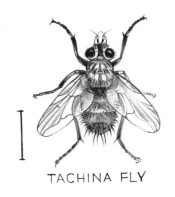

TACHINA FLY

WARBLE FLY

EGGS ON HAIR

COW'S HOOF

LARVA

LARVA UNDER SKIN

When I see our cows run
and kick their heels in the air,
I know they're being bothered
by warble flies. They lay
their eggs mostly on the heels
and legs of the cows. When the eggs
hatch, the little larvas burrow
into their flesh, and that's very painful.

PYRGOTA FLY

I like to hunt for beetles under the
street lights. One night I saw
a big beetle leave with a
small fly on its back. That fly is
going to lay an egg under the skin
of the beetle. In a few days the egg
will hatch and the young larva
will feast on fresh beetle.

Flesh flies skim over the meadow
sipping nectar from the flowers.
The female's eggs hatch
inside her body. She will attack
a grasshopper that's flying
and make it fall on the ground.
Then she puts her larvas on it
and they'll have food as they grow.

The mydas fly is a large, handsome fly.
I like the bright orange belt
he wears around his body.
He's found all over North America,
usually around decaying wood
where there are beetle larvas to eat.

MYDAS
FLY

HUMPBACKED FLY

I saw a humpbacked fly
on the kitchen window one night.
I could see the shape of its
hump clearly with my hand lens.
It flies quickly, with jerks.
When a female finds a caterpillar,
she lays her eggs on its body.

The black and yellow syrphid flies
are called flower flies.
As they leave each flower, they carry
away a bit of pollen to another
flower. That's what makes
fruit and seeds for another year.
The farmers are happy to have the
flower flies in their fruit orchards.

FLOWER
FLY

On some days I find the meadow
alive with colorful soldier flies.
Their black bodies are striped with
yellow like a soldier's uniform.
They fly from flower to flower
sipping nectar and scattering pollen
along the way.

SOLDIER FLY

We have a big walnut tree
in our back yard. This year
some pretty little flies
appeared on the walnuts.
The walnut husks turned black
and squashy. They were wet
and messy. This little fly would be
a terrible pest in a big nut orchard.

WALNUT HUSK
FLY

The windowpane fly is a great
traveler. It's found
all over North America and most of
the world. It seems to travel
on ships loaded with grain and flour.
I often see it on the windows
of the mill in our town.

FLOUR

WINDOWPANE FLY

I like to run barefooted
on the beach. As I pass a pile
of kelp, I pull out a long strand
of seaweed. A huge swarm
of little gray flies comes out
into the air. What a noise they make!
I watch them settle back into the kelp,
then I run on to the next pile.

KELP FLY

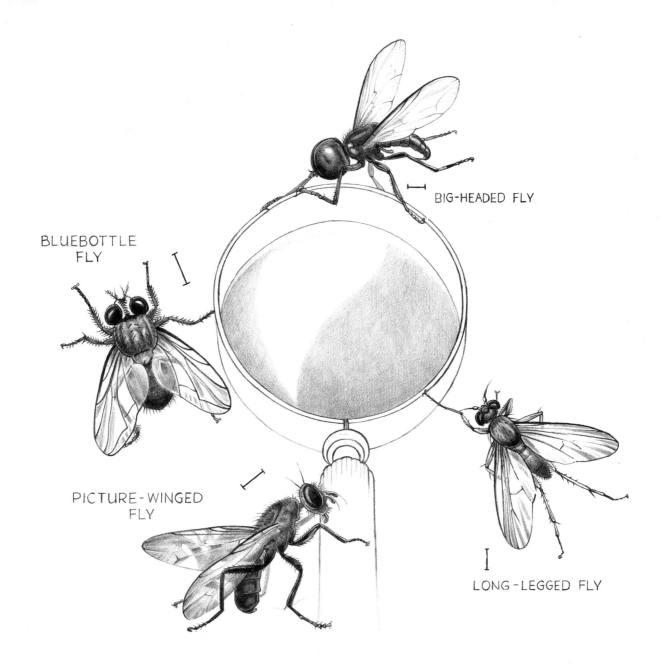

BIG-HEADED FLY

BLUEBOTTLE
FLY

PICTURE-WINGED
FLY

LONG-LEGGED FLY

There are lots more kinds of flies around.
I'm going to keep looking for them.